WHO ELSE IN HISTORY?

Hidden Heroes in
THE CIVIL WAR

Elliott Smith

Lerner Publications ◆ Minneapolis

Lerner Publications Company
An imprint of Lerner Publishing Group, Inc.
241 First Avenue North
Minneapolis, MN 55401 USA

For reading levels and more information, look up this title at www.lernerbooks.com.

Main body text set in Aptifer Sans LT Pro.
Typeface provided by Linotype AG.

Editor: Brianna Kaiser **Designer:** Viet Chu **Photo Editor:** Cynthia Zemlicka

Library of Congress Cataloging-in-Publication Data

Names: Smith, Elliott, 1976– author.
Title: Hidden heroes in the Civil War / Elliott Smith.
Description: Minneapolis, MN: Lerner Publications, [2023] | Series: Who else in history? (alternator books ®) | Includes bibliographical references and index. | Audience: Ages 8–12 | Audience: Grades 4–6 | Summary: "Personal accounts of nurses, soldiers, and more tell the stories of unfamiliar figures of the US Civil War. Learn about the women, people of color, and others who played a crucial role in the war"—Provided by publisher.
Identifiers: LCCN 2021035567 | ISBN 9781728458397 (library binding) | ISBN 9781728464046 (paperback) | ISBN 9781728462585 (ebook)
Subjects: LCSH: United States—History—Civil War, 1861–1865—Anecdotes—Juvenile literature. | United States—History—Civil War, 1861–1865—Biography—Juvenile literature.
Classification: LCC E655 .S74 2023 | DDC 973.7—dc23

LC record available at https://lccn.loc.gov/2021035567

Manufactured in the United States of America
1-50868-50205-11/12/2021

TABLE OF CONTENTS

JOURNEY TO FREEDOM

Robert Smalls longed for freedom. He was an enslaved person living in South Carolina, a state where slavery was permitted. But the Civil War (1861–1865) was changing the course of the nation. The Union, made up of Northern states, fought to end slavery in the US. The Confederacy, made up of Southern states, fought to keep slavery.

Many people of color, including Black men of the Fourth US Colored Infantry, fought for the Union during the Civil War.

Robert Smalls

On May 12, 1862, twenty-three-year-old Smalls was working on the USS *Planter*, a Confederate ship. That night Smalls and the crew took control after the captain and officers left the ship to go into town. They sailed the *Planter* up the coast and stopped along the way to pick up their families.

Smalls sailed the ship to Union ships near Fort Sumter early on May 13. He delivered the Confederate weapons that were on board his ship to the Union army. Smalls had guided seventeen people to freedom. He was honored by the navy and later fought for the Union.

Smalls's story is one of many that is often not discussed in teachings of the Civil War. People from underrepresented groups made great contributions to the war, and their stories often go untold.

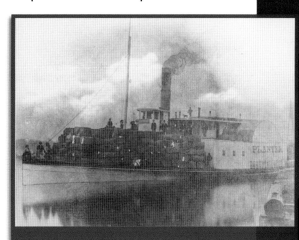
The USS *Planter* was built in South Carolina in 1860.

STRONG VOICES

Before the war started, many people fought to stop slavery. Two abolitionists were among those who helped turn public opinion against slavery, especially in the North.

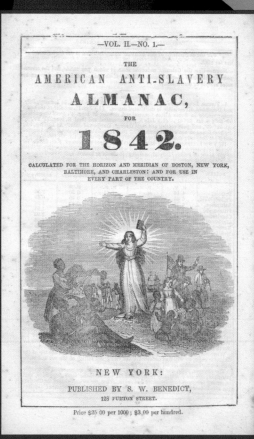

The 1842 (*left*) and 1843 (*right*) editions of the *American Anti-Slavery Almanac*, published by the American Anti-Slavery Society

HENRY HIGHLAND GARNET

Henry Highland Garnet was born into slavery. When he was nine, his family escaped to the North for freedom. Garnet grew interested in religion and later became a minister. He was also passionate about ending slavery. He joined the American Anti-Slavery Society and used his speaking talent to argue for the end of slavery.

Henry Highland Garnet continued working as a minister after the war ended.

At an 1843 convention in New York, Garnet delivered a speech titled "Call to Rebellion." He argued that the only way Black people would be free is through fighting their oppressors. He said those enslaved should "rather die freemen, than live to be slaves."

Many in the abolitionist movement disagreed with Garnet. But Garnet continued to fight for the end of slavery. He later recruited Black soldiers to join the Union army. On February 12, 1865, he became the first Black minister to deliver a sermon to the US Congress.

LUCRETIA MOTT

Lucretia Mott became one of the loudest female voices in the abolitionist movement. During that time, people were not supportive of women speaking publicly. But Mott was confident in her message and spent her life speaking out against injustice.

In 1833 she helped form the Philadelphia Female Anti-Slavery Society. The organization fought for emancipation, established a school for Black students, and supported antislavery newspapers and conventions.

Mott continued to face opposition. But she helped a number of escaped fugitives, all while lecturing across the world. Later in life, she continued advocating for the rights of women and Black people.

Lucretia Mott was one of the founders of the Philadelphia Female Anti-Slavery Society. The group ended in 1870.

A group of abolitionists, including Frederick Douglass, Emily Edmonson, and Mary Edmonson, attend a convention in August 1850.

CRITICAL THINKING

Why do you think it was important for abolitionists to raise public awareness against slavery?

A HELPING HAND

Money was needed to support the abolitionist movement. Producing newspapers or helping the newly free land on their feet could be costly. Sometimes money came from a surprising source.

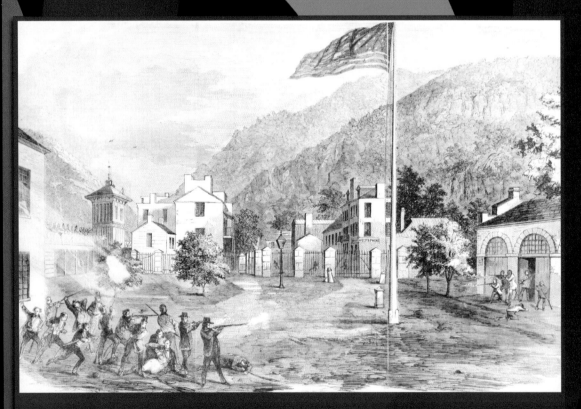

This illustration from November 5, 1859, shows John Brown's raid on Harpers Ferry.

MARY ELLEN PLEASANT

Mary Ellen Pleasant fought for civil rights. She also helped get better housing and education for Black people.

Mary Ellen Pleasant was a mysterious figure. People don't know for certain where she was born or if she was enslaved. But we know she was a powerful benefactor to those fighting against slavery.

Pleasant married James Smith in the 1840s, and the couple worked together on the Underground Railroad. When Smith died, he left Pleasant a lot of money.

She used her money to invest in businesses and to fund the fight against slavery. In 1859 she aided abolitionist John Brown's raid at Harpers Ferry, then in Virginia. Brown took over the weapons storage at Harpers Ferry, hoping the local enslaved population would join him and revolt. But the mission failed and Brown was captured.

"My cause was the cause of freedom and equality for myself and for my people and I'd rather be a corpse than a coward."

—MARY ELLEN PLEASANT

HEALING HANDS

Great strides were made in health care during the Civil War. During the war, most nurses and doctors were white men. But some people worked to change that.

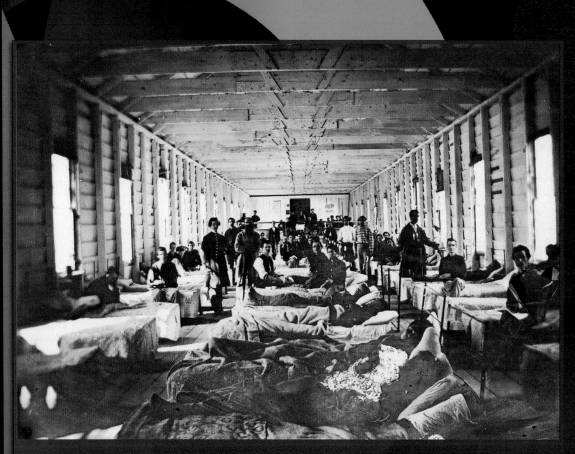

Soldiers are treated at Camp Convalescent in Alexandria, Virginia.

Dorothea Dix is a social reformer who made important contributions to the nursing field.

DOROTHEA DIX

Dorothea Dix was named superintendent of nurses for the Union army. She brought thousands of nurses into the field, providing critical help for wounded soldiers. Dix fought to get her nurses better pay, housing, and transportation. She also fought for social reform throughout her life and fought for better care for people experiencing mental illness.

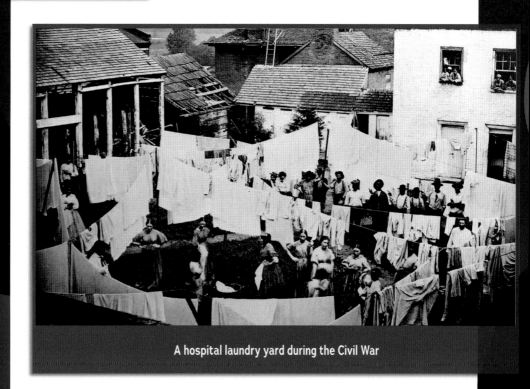

A hospital laundry yard during the Civil War

Susie King Taylor is the only Black woman to publish a Civil War memoir.

SUSIE KING TAYLOR

Susie King Taylor, born Susan Baker, was the first Black nurse during the Civil War. She was born into slavery in Georgia. Georgia had laws forbidding the education of Black people. But Taylor was taught in secret by Black women. She became free at fourteen.

Taylor treated Black soldiers at a hospital in South Carolina for more than four years, without pay. While an army nurse, she taught her Black peers how to read and write. Taylor published a book in 1902 about her experiences.

"I was very happy to know my efforts were successful in camp, and also felt grateful for the appreciation of my services."

—SUSIE KING TAYLOR, CIVIL WAR MEMOIR

ALEXANDER AUGUSTA

Alexander Augusta always wanted to be a doctor. However, due to racial discrimination in the United States, he wasn't accepted into any US colleges. So in 1850, he decided to attend Trinity College in Canada, where he earned his medical degree in 1856.

In the early 1860s, he moved back to the US and wrote a letter to President Abraham Lincoln, offering his services as a doctor in the war. Lincoln agreed and Augusta became the first Black surgeon in the US Army. He later became a major. But when several white doctors complained about taking orders from Augusta, he was reassigned to the Freedmen's Hospital in Washington, DC.

In March 1865, Augusta received the rank of lieutenant colonel. After the Civil War ended, he taught at Howard University and continued to practice medicine.

Alexander Augusta is the first Black person to earn the title of lieutenant colonel.

BEHIND ENEMY LINES

The Civil War pitted friends and neighbors against one another. Relationships were strained between those who supported slavery and those who were against it.

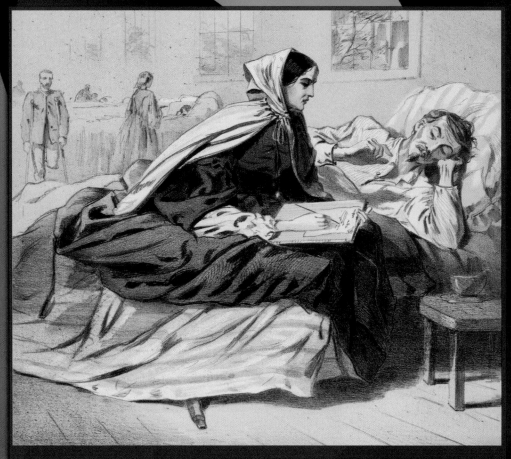

Women assisted in the Civil War in many ways, including visiting wounded soldiers.

Although Eliza Potter lived in an area where most people supported the Confederacy, Potter supported the Union.

ELIZA POTTER

Eliza Potter and her family were well liked in Charleston, South Carolina. But when the war began and the Potters' support of the Union became known, they were outcasts.

Potter stayed strong in her beliefs. She spent time and money helping wounded Union soldiers behind enemy lines. Often these men were left to die, as Confederate doctors rarely attended to them.

After the war, Potter had two monuments built at Beaufort National Cemetery. On the base of one monument are the names of 175 Union soldiers Potter took care of as a nurse.

CRITICAL THINKING

Why is it important to do what you think is right, even if everyone else around you disagrees?

ON THE FRONT LINES

These are some of the many people who fought for the Union army to take a stand for what they believed in.

In 1864 Ah Yee Way rescued his regiment's flag during the Battle of Spotsylvania Court House.

AH YEE WAY

Ah Yee Way, also called Thomas Sylvanus, was brought to America from China as a child for an education and was enslaved in Baltimore in the mid-1850s. At the beginning of the Civil War, when he was about sixteen, he ran away and joined the Union army.

He was partially blinded in his first battle and was discharged, but he reenlisted twice and served in the army until May 1865. At the Battle of Spotsylvania Court House in 1864, he rescued his regiment's flag after his comrades were wounded. Later in the Civil War, he was captured and held in Andersonville (also called Camp Sumter), a Confederate military prison in Georgia, for nine months. He died on June 15, 1891, at the age of forty-five.

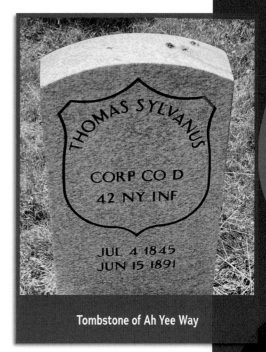

Tombstone of Ah Yee Way

JOSEPH DE CASTRO

Joseph De Castro was born in Boston in 1844. He joined the Union army in 1861, signing up for the Nineteenth Massachusetts Infantry. He was a flag-bearer.

Joseph De Castro was awarded the Medal of Honor for his actions during Pickett's Charge.

A Civil War Medal of Honor

On July 3, 1863, the last day of the Battle of Gettysburg, the Confederate army launched an assault on the Union army, called Pickett's Charge. During the fight, De Castro captured the Virginia flag. He was awarded the Medal of Honor, the highest medal that can be given to a member of the armed forces, for his heroism. De Castro was the first Hispanic soldier to receive the award.

An engraving of Pickett's Charge at the Battle of Gettysburg

SARAH EDMONDS SEELYE

Sarah Edmonds Seelye disguised herself as Franklin Thompson during the Civil War.

Sarah Edmonds Seelye was born in Canada. In 1857, when she was a teenager, she ran away to the US to flee an abusive father. To avoid being found, she disguised herself as a man. Four years later, Edmonds enlisted in the Union army disguised as Franklin Thompson.

She served as a mail carrier and hospital attendant. She also served as a spy. But when she contracted malaria in 1863, Edmonds fled camp for fear of being discovered. Franklin Thompson was charged with desertion, leaving military duty without returning.

After leaving the army, Edmonds fought to get her army pension. But since Franklin Thompson had been charged with desertion, she was not eligible for the money. With the help of her former regiment, she was able to get her desertion charges cleared and full pension restored in 1884.

Seelye helped the Union retreat during the Battle of Bull Run on July 21, 1861. She also nursed wounded soldiers from the battle.

RIGHT-HAND MAN

Many people, such as Abraham Lincoln, are very well-known figures of the Civil War. However, these well-known figures often worked with people who did not get credit for their contribution in the fight for freedom.

A sketch from *Frank Leslie's Illustrated Almanac* of the Second Louisiana Native Guard in battle

Ely Parker

Ely Parker during the Civil War

Ely Parker was a member of the Seneca, an Iroquois Nation. He wanted to be a lawyer but was not allowed to take the required exam due to discrimination against Indigenous people. With his dreams of being a lawyer dashed, he turned to engineering. His work on a government project in Galena, Illinois, led him to meeting Union army general Ulysses S. Grant.

Ulysses S. Grant (*center*) and members of his staff (*from left*) Ely Parker, Adam Dadeau, Orville Elias Babcock, and Horace Porter

During the Civil War, Parker worked as Grant's military secretary. By the end of the war, Parker rose to the rank of lieutenant colonel. In 1865 he drafted the terms of the Confederate surrender at Appomattox.

In 1869 Parker was named the commissioner of Indian Affairs, the first Indigenous person to hold the position.

Parker with other members of Grant's staff

REMEMBERING THE UNSUNG HEROES

These are not the only unsung heroes of the Civil War. André Cailloux was one of the first Black officers in the Union Army. Mary Bowser used her photographic memory to spy on Confederate president Jefferson Davis for the Union. Cailloux, Bowser, and others played a role in changing the country for the better during the difficult era of slavery and the Civil War.

An 1863 depiction of the funeral of André Cailloux, who died during combat in the war

TIMELINE

1833: Lucretia Mott helps form the Philadelphia Female Anti-Slavery Society.

1843: Henry Highland Garnet's controversial "Call to Rebellion" speech says enslaved people should fight for their freedom.

1859: Mary Ellen Pleasant helps fund John Brown's raid on Harpers Ferry.

1861: Dorothea Dix is named superintendent of army nurses in June.

Sarah Edmonds Seelye enters the Union army in May as Franklin Thompson.

Ah Yee Way enlists in the Union army in August.

1862: Robert Smalls takes the *Planter* and sails it to waiting Union soldiers.

1863: Joseph De Castro captures the Confederate flag at the Battle of Gettysburg.

1865: Alexander Augusta achieves the rank of lieutenant colonel in March.

Ely Parker writes the articles of surrender, ending the Civil War in April.

1870: One of Eliza Potter's monuments is constructed at Beaufort National Cemetery.

1902: Susie King Taylor publishes her memoir about working as a Black nurse in the war.

Glossary

benefactor: someone who helps another, especially by providing money

discharge: to release from military duty

enlist: to sign up to serve in the military

fugitive: a person who is escaping or running away

Indigenous: the first people who lived in any region

monument: a structure made to keep the memory of a person or event alive

oppressor: a person who uses power in a cruel or unfair way

outcast: one who is driven out or rejected by society

pension: a sum paid regularly to a person who is retired from work

regiment: a troop of soldiers made up of at least two battalions

Source Notes

7 "Garnet's 'Call to Rebellion.'" PBS, August 21, 1843, https://www.pbs.org/wgbh/aia/part4/4h2937t.html.

11 Liza Veale, "The Real History behind Mary Ellen Pleasant, San Francisco's 'Voodoo Queen,'" KALW, September 9, 2015, https://www.kalw.org/show/crosscurrents/2015-09-09/the-real-history-behind-mary-ellen-pleasant-san-franciscos-voodoo-queen.

14 "Susie King Taylor," Library of Congress, accessed August 8, 2021, https://www.loc.gov/ghe/cascade/index.html?appid=5be2377c246c4b5483e32ddd51d32dc0&bookmark=Forgotten%20Heroes.

Learn More

African-American Soldiers during the Civil War
https://www.loc.gov/classroom-materials/united-states-history
-primary-source-timeline/civil-war-and-reconstruction-1861-1877
/african-american-soldiers-during-the-civil-war/

American Civil War
https://kids.britannica.com/kids/article/American-Civil-War/352967

Bruchac, Joseph. *One Real American: The Life of Ely S. Parker, Seneca Sachem and Civil War General*. New York: Abrams Books for Young Readers, 2020.

Halfmann, Janet. *The Story of Civil War Hero Robert Smalls*. New York: Lee & Low Books, 2020.

Huddleston, Emma. *Civil War Spy Stories*. Mankato, MN: Child's World, 2020.

Smith, Elliott. *Abolitionism: The Movement to End Slavery*. Minneapolis: Lerner Publications, 2022.

Spies
https://www.nps.gov/civilwar/spies.htm

Women amidst War
https://www.nps.gov/civilwar/women-amidst-war.htm

Index

Photo Acknowledgments

Image credits: Library of Congress, pp. 4, 5 (left), 10, 14, 18, 21 (left), 25 (bottom), 29 (top), 29 (bottom); U.S. Naval History and Heritage Command Photograph, p. 5 (right); Smithsonian National Museum of African American History and Culture, p. 6 (left); Wikimedia Commons, pp. 6 (right), 21 (right); National Portrait Gallery, Smithsonian Institution, pp. 7, 8, 28; Fotosearch/Getty Images/Getty Images, pp. 9, 22; Everett/Shutterstock, p. 11; Heritage Images/Getty Images, p. 12; FLHC 90/Alamy Stock Photo, p. 13 (top); Corbis/Getty Images, p. 13 (bottom); National Library of Medicine, p. 15; *The Letter for Home* (Campaign Sketches) by Winslow Homer. Public domain via National Gallery of Art, p. 16; U.S. Department of Veterans Affairs, National Cemetery Administration, p. 17; Julie Krol/Find a Grave, p. 19; Niday Picture Library/Alamy Stock Photo, p. 20; AP Photo/Free Lance-Star, p. 23; Buyenlarge/Getty Images, p. 24; National Archives, pp. 25, 26; *Harpers Weekly*, August 29, 1863, p. 27. Design element: filo/Getty Images.

Cover: Oblate Sisters of Providence Archives, Baltimore, Maryland (Alexander T. Augusta); Fotosearch/Getty Images (Sarah Edmonds); Library of Congress (Susie King Taylor).